RD WILDLIFE

Squirrels

by Derek Zobel

BELLWETHER MEDIA • MINNEAPOLIS, MN

Note to Librarians, Teachers, and Parents:

Blastoff! Readers are carefully developed by literacy experts and combine standards-based content with developmentally appropriate text.

Level 1 provides the most support through repetition of high-frequency words, light text, predictable sentence patterns, and strong visual support.

Level 2 offers early readers a bit more challenge through varied simple sentences, increased text load, and less repetition of high-frequency words.

Level 3 advances early-fluent readers toward fluency through increased text and concept load, less reliance on visuals, longer sentences, and more literary language.

Level 4 builds reading stamina by providing more text per page, increased use of punctuation, greater variation in sentence patterns, and increasingly challenging vocabulary.

Level 5 encourages children to move from "learning to read" to "reading to learn" by providing even more text, varied writing styles, and less familiar topics.

Whichever book is right for your reader, Blastoff! Readers are the perfect books to build confidence and encourage a love of reading that will last a lifetime!

This edition first published in 2011 by Bellwether Media, Inc.

No part of this publication may be reproduced in whole or in part without written permission of the publisher. For information regarding permission, write to Bellwether Media, Inc., Attention: Permissions Department, 5357 Penn Avenue South, Minneapolis, MN 55419.

Library of Congress Cataloging-in-Publication Data
Zobel, Derek, 1983–
Squirrels / by Derek Zobel.
  p. cm. – (Blastoff! readers. Backyard wildlife)
Summary: "Developed by literacy experts for students in kindergarten through grade three, this book introduces squirrels to young readers through leveled text and related photos"–Provided by publisher.
Includes bibliographical references and index.
ISBN 978-1-60014-447-9 (hardcover : alk. paper)
1. Squirrels–Juvenile literature. I. Title.
QL737.R68Z69 2010
599.36–dc22   2010010684

Printed in the United States of America, North Mankato, MN.
080110   1162

Contents

What Are Squirrels? 4

Squirrel Teeth 10

What Squirrels Eat 16

Staying Safe 18

Glossary 22

To Learn More 23

Index 24

Squirrels are **rodents**. They live in grasslands, forests, and deserts.

Big, bushy tails help squirrels **balance** when they climb trees.

Squirrels have sharp **claws**. Claws help squirrels grip trees.

Squirrels have
four teeth.
Their teeth never
stop growing.

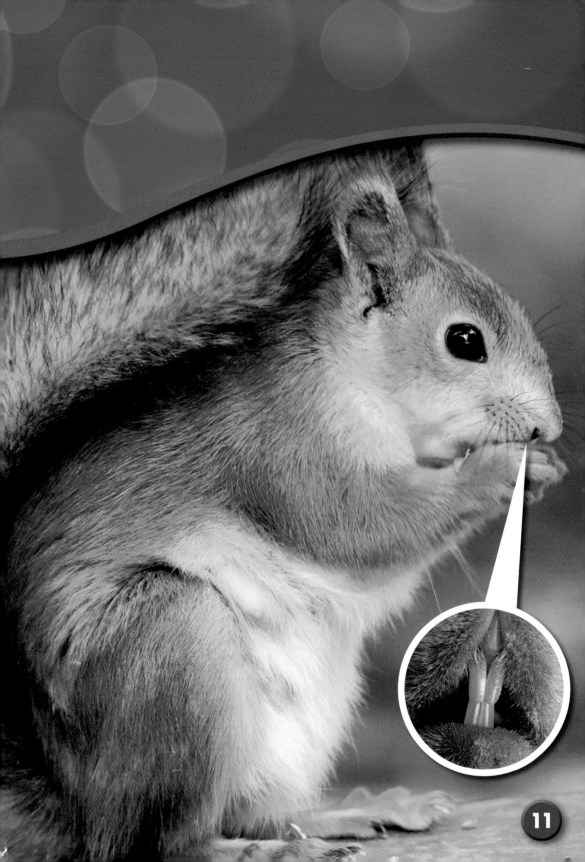

Squirrels **gnaw** on food to wear down their teeth.

Squirrels also chew on branches to clean their teeth.

Squirrels eat nuts, leaves, **insects**, and fruits. They also eat bark in the winter.

Squirrels have big
eyes to watch
for **predators**.

Squirrels run to their
nests or **burrows**
to stay safe.
Get inside quickly!

Glossary

balance—to stay steady and not fall

burrows—tunnels squirrels dig and live in

claws—nails on the feet of squirrels; claws help squirrels climb.

gnaw—to bite or nibble on something for a long time

insects—small animals with six legs and hard outer bodies; insect bodies are divided into three parts.

predators—animals that hunt other animals for food

rodents—a group of small animals that usually gnaw on their food

To Learn More

AT THE LIBRARY

Diemer, Lauren. *Squirrels*. New York, N.Y.:
Weigl Publishers, 2008.

Ehlert, Lois. *Nuts to You!* Orlando, Fla.:
Voyager Books, 2004.

Swanson, Diane. *Squirrels*. Milwaukee, Wisc.:
Gareth Stevens Publishing, 2003.

ON THE WEB

Learning more about squirrels
is as easy as 1, 2, 3.

1. Go to www.factsurfer.com.

2. Enter "squirrels" into the search box.

3. Click the "Surf" button and you will see a
   list of related Web sites.

With factsurfer.com, finding more information
is just a click away.

Index

balance, 6
bark, 16
branches, 14
burrows, 20
chew, 14
claws, 8
clean, 14
climb, 6
deserts, 4
eyes, 18
food, 12
forests, 4
fruits, 16
gnaw, 12
grasslands, 4
grip, 8
growing, 10

insects, 16
inside, 20
leaves, 16
nests, 20
nuts, 16
predators, 18
quickly, 20
rodents, 4
run, 20
safe, 20
tails, 6
teeth, 10, 12, 14
trees, 6, 8
watch, 18
wear, 12
winter, 16